Smoke-Free And No Buts!

by

Dr Geoff Ibbotson
&
Dr Ann Williamson

Illustrated
by
Martin Hughes

Crown House Publishing Limited

First published in the UK by

Crown House Publishing Ltd
Crown Buildings
Bancyfelin
Carmarthen
Wales

British Library of Cataloguing-in-Publication Data
A catalogue entry for this book is available
from the British Library.

ISBN 1899836209

Printed and bound in Wales by
WBC Book Manufacturers,
Waterton Industrial Estate,
Bridgend, Mid Glamorgan.

Dedication

We would like to dedicate this book to the memory of our friend and mentor Dr Pat Brown from Ireland whose wisdom, insight and encouragement were a source of inspiration to us and many others.

About The Authors

Dr Ann Williamson is a GP with twenty-five years' experience in practice. She has been using hypnosis to facilitate change and empower her patients for nearly ten years. An ex-smoker herself, she is married with three children and lives where she practises, in a small Lancashire town on the edge of the Pennines.

Dr Geoff Ibbotson was a GP for twenty-two years before he left his practice to pursue his interests in Chest Medicine and in the applications of hypnosis. He works in the Chest Clinic at Fazakerley Hospital, Liverpool, and also in the Clinical Psychology Department at Fairfield Hospital, Bury, as well as practising hypnotherapy on a private basis.

Both Geoff and Ann are accredited members of the British Society of Medical & Dental Hypnosis and certified NLP Master Practitioners who have also been involved with teaching doctors and dentists how to use hypnotic techniques for themselves and within their own practices. Also, they run stress management and personal development workshops under the title **Dynamic Education and Training.** They can be contacted at: ann.williamson@zen.co.uk

Contents

Acknowledgements

Throughout the years we have been taught many things by many people. It is impossible to acknowledge and individually thank all those whose work has gone before. We would therefore like to thank all those who have played a part in the development of our conscious and unconscious learning over the years.

Martin Hughes from the depths of Walsall, near Birmingham, is responsible for the cartoons in this book and our thanks go to him and our friend Charles Eveniss who put us in touch with each other and was the inspiration for some of the cartoon figures!

We would also like to thank Ann's husband, Iain, who has adjusted our grammar and corrected our spelling mistakes along the way.

Chapter One

How Can I Become An Ex-Smoker?

Everyone knows all the good reasons against smoking and many people say that they would like to stop if only they could. This book will help you to have the choice of becoming an ex-smoker if you want to. We have used these techniques for some years now and they are so successful that we have felt motivated to write this book.

Stopping smoking and not starting again are two totally different processes and each needs specific strategies. If you have previously tried and failed in your smoking cessation then now is a good time to honestly evaluate your reasons for failure. You will then be in a position to regard your previous attempts as a learning process rather than a failure, and thence move on to successfully become an ex-smoker.

There are two components to the dependence on smoking: physical dependence on nicotine, and psychological dependence on the process of smoking. If one wishes to break two sticks then it is much easier to separate them before attempting to break them. In the same way it is much easier to deal with these two elements separately.

The physical addiction can be tackled by reducing the amount you smoke gradually. Turning to cigars or pipes usually worsens the situation as previous cigarette smokers tend to inhale the cigar or pipe smoke with its much higher level of nicotine and tar.

The psychological benefits you gain from smoking need to be assessed, and a better way of satisfying these needs to be found. We teach you ways that you can successfully tackle this.

The behaviour of smoking functions as an unconscious process or automatic habit and is therefore difficult to stop. We will use techniques to bring it into consciousness and then break up the habit pattern.

There is a saying, "The road is smooth... why do you throw rocks before you?" We are going to turn that principle to our advantage. If we do NOT wish to travel on the road, would it not be a good idea to throw some rocks or even boulders in front of us? As well as bringing the smoking into consciousness we should also make it extremely inconvenient.

Then when we actually stop completely, it comes as quite a relief!

Whose Idea Is It To Stop?
Let's just review who wants you to stop. Is it yourself or is it an instruction which is given by others? If you honestly want to stop because it is your idea, then that's fine – read on!

If you have been strongly advised to stop on medical grounds then let's look at the situation. Whose health is at risk if you continue to smoke? We are sure that you realise that your continuing to smoke will not harm the health of whoever has advised you to stop. If you are uncertain of the reason you were advised to stop, then look at that and be quite clear about the risks of continuing to smoke. You will then probably be in the state of wishing you could stop, and hoping you can. That's fine; we will help you, through this book, to turn your wish into reality.

So you really don't want to stop at this stage? That is your prerogative. We are not going to bully you and tell you that you must stop now. If you do not stop, then the process has not failed.

Perhaps you are uncertain as to whether you really wish to stop completely now. Well, that's fine, too. Perhaps you would like to start the process of reduction and bringing the process into consciousness now, and then, at some time in the future, when you wish to stop completely, you will be in a better position with greater control over your habit.

Why Do I Smoke?
Have you have ever sat down and really thought about why you smoke – not just in general, but the reason for smoking each particular cigarette?

As you have decided to become an ex-smoker, you first need to become aware of why you smoke each cigarette, so that you can satisfy that need in some other way.

Some people find that they smoke to relieve stress or boredom. Sometimes you may find that you are using smoking to help your self-confidence – to give yourself something to do with your hands in a social situation you find difficult. At other times smoking may be just pure habit – because you always have had a cigarette with your cup of coffee, you automatically light up in that situation.

4

Why Can't I Just Stop?

So you have decided to become an ex-smoker... Have you ever wondered why you have not been able to stop before? ...surely you can just decide what you want to do and then do it! ...or can you?

We would like to introduce you, at this point, to a useful model that may help to explain why this is so often difficult.

A model is not the 'truth' but an explanation based on what we know so far that helps us to understand what might be happening.

The brain has two halves which tend to function fairly independently.

The left half of the brain, which is responsible for our verbal and arithmetical skills, and is the source of our critical, evaluative, logical thought processes, is that part of our mind or consciousness that we generally use most in our day-to-day activity.

The right side of our brain, which becomes more active as we relax, is responsible for our visual and creative imagination, our intuitive and instinctive part of ourselves, and is the source of our feelings and emotions.

Normally there is little communication between these two halves, e.g. the left brain knows many good logical reasons why one should not smoke but the right brain wants a smoke (feeling), and whenever there is conflict between right and left brain the right side nearly always wins.

Simply deciding at a logical level that you want to be an ex-smoker, and then expecting to be able to achieve this, is about as effective as telling someone 'not to worry' when they are experiencing a panic attack. Logical reasoning doesn't get through very well in the normal waking state to that part of our consciousness where we process our feelings.

To successfully set yourself the goal of becoming an ex-smoker and then achieve it, you need to get in touch with that part of your mind where you keep the feeling of wanting to smoke.

Over the next few chapters we will show you how to do just that.

Chapter Two

Getting In Touch With Your
Unconscious Mind

As we mentioned earlier, when in our normal waking state our brain functions predominantly in a 'left brain' mode. As you begin to relax the activity begins to shift over to the 'right brain'. The critical, evaluative thought processes (predominantly a left brain or conscious operation) start to lessen, and suggestions are more easily accepted.

This shift in brain activity occurs quite naturally throughout our day anyway. Whenever we find ourselves gazing out of the window in a daydream; driving on 'auto-pilot', with no conscious recollection of the last few miles; whenever we become totally focused in an activity and lose awareness of our surroundings, we are predominantly in a 'right brain' state.

What we want to teach you is how to access this state of mind, whenever you wish it; to bring it under your own conscious control, so that you can utilise it to help you achieve your goals.

How Can I Do That?

There are many different ways to increase your right brain activity, and we will describe a few. Try them out and see which one feels right for you. We all have differences in how we experience reality, so what you need to do is to find your own personal 'key' to open the 'door' to your 'unconscious' right brain.

As we start to relax or increase 'right brain' activity, we can in this way start to access our 'unconscious' mind and thus begin to affect how we feel about smoking. We can also begin to accept suggestions that will help us alter our smoking behaviour. To continue the metaphor, once through the 'door' you can begin to reorganise or tidy up the room.

Remember that, as our right brain 'thinks' in pictures, using imagery and visualisation is an effective way to access our right brain or 'unconscious' mind. However, not everyone is good at imagining pictures in their mind's eye in glorious 3-D technicolour! This doesn't really matter because when you think of something, or you are aware of something, you are making an image or representation at some level in your mind. How do you recognise a chair as a chair unless you compare what you see to some internal image that you have labelled as a chair? So, in this book, if we suggest that you visualise something, don't feel you actually need to 'see' a picture ...just allow yourself to have an awareness.

Safety Rules – OK?

Whenever you decide to sit down and use a formal self-hypnotic or relaxation technique there are a few precautions that it is wise to take. Always tell yourself before you start how long you want to relax for, because when you become practised at doing these types of exercises you may get quite deeply relaxed and experience time distortion. You may feel you have only been relaxing for ten minutes and half an hour may have passed. This could be very inconvenient, so tell your unconscious mind how long you want and trust it to give you notice when that time has elapsed.

If you are overtired, any relaxation technique may send you to sleep so, if this is not desirable, make sure you have turned on an alarm before you start.

Never use these techniques in the driving seat of a car as you don't want to link a relaxed hypnotic state with sitting in the driver's seat. Always move over to the passenger seat. Become used to getting into a relaxed state both while sitting or lying down.

Only use these techniques when it is safe and appropriate to do so.

If an emergency occurs whilst you are relaxing you can get up immediately and deal with it, but, as you focus internally, your awareness of what is going on outside you becomes less. You can still hear sounds around you, but they become less intrusive.

What Is It Like?

Everyone is different and so each person will experience a trance-like state differently. You may feel relaxed, and that can be very enjoyable, but you don't have to feel relaxed. An athlete focusing internally before a race is far from relaxed but still in that trance-like 'right brain' state.

Some people experience a feeling of heaviness, some a feeling of lightness, some may feel warm and tingly, others may lose awareness of where their arms and legs are resting. Whatever you feel is fine, and right for you.

Some people find getting into 'right brain' activity easier than others but, as with any skill, it can improve with practice. We would recommend that, if this is unfamiliar to you, you practise for five or ten minutes, maybe twice a day, for the first three to four weeks.

The time spent in this way is more than made up for by your improved effectiveness and concentration, as you feel less stressed or anxious and become the master rather than the victim of your emotions.

A Self-Hypnotic Technique

One popular way of achieving this relaxed, trance-like state is by using a progressive muscular relaxation such as that described next. You could read it through and then see whether this particular method suits you. You might find it easier to read it into a cassette recorder and then listen to it whilst following the instructions.

A Progressive Muscular Relaxation Technique

Perhaps you would like to make yourself comfortable, place your feet firmly on the floor, and let your hands just rest easily on your lap. If you prefer, you could lie down somewhere comfortable.

I would like you now to take a deep breath in, and as you breathe out, just let your body go loose and slack, like a rag doll.

Just let all the tensions drain away with each outgoing breath.

As you breathe out you can let your eyes close and focus on the muscles of your head and face and neck.

Let the muscles of your head and face and neck go loose and slack. Become aware of your forehead, very wide and smooth. Become aware of the space within your mouth, of the position of your tongue. Notice the muscles of your throat relax as you swallow.

You might like to imagine a colour or a warm glow drifting down your body from the top of your head as you begin to relax.

Let a feeling of comfort drift gently down into your neck and shoulders. Let the muscles around your shoulders go loose and slack; let the relaxation drift down your arms right to your fingertips.

Let your arms feel heavy and comfortable. You might notice a tingling feeling or a feeling of warmth in your hands as they relax.

Let the muscles around your chest relax, let the feeling of comfort spread down into the muscles of your back and stomach and let the muscles of your tummy go loose and slack as that colour drifts down.

Let any outside noises just recede into the background and contribute to a feeling of safety and comfort.

Enjoy just being, instead of having to be doing.

Let the muscles of your legs go loose and slack, let them feel really heavy, sinking down like two lead weights to the floor as the relaxation spreads down, right down to your toes. Let the tensions drain out of the soles of your feet into the floor.

Become aware of your breathing; maybe imagining breathing in a colour and noticing it spreading throughout your body as you relax, letting go of any tension as you breathe out.

Just enjoy that lovely comfortable feeling, letting go with each outgoing breath to become just as deeply relaxed as you want to be.

A Special Place
I would like you now to imagine a very special place, a place where you can feel completely relaxed and safe and calm.
Let your conscious mind wonder what place your unconscious mind will find for you.

It may be a place you have visited before or it may be a place that your mind finds for you. It may be inside or outside.

Look all around you, notice the colours, whatever you can see.

Smell any smells that might be there.

Hear any sounds that might be in the place you have chosen, and look to see where they are coming from.

Begin to notice the texture of what you are standing or resting on, the temperature of the air around you. Above all feel the peace and calmness of the place you have chosen.

Really experience this special place, because this is your own special place that no-one can take from you, a place where you can go to when you need to relax, to recharge your batteries, a place where any suggestions you give yourself will sink straight into your unconscious mind and begin to exert an effect on how you think and how you feel and how you behave.

Each time you use these techniques it will become easier to become even more relaxed, even more quickly.

Coming back to the here and now
Enjoy those feelings of relaxation and calmness and, in a few minutes, when you are ready, you can gradually come back to the here and now.

You can count yourself back in your head from 5 to 1, taking the time you need, so that by the time you reach 1 you are wide awake, feeling refreshed and alert with all your sensations back to normal but keeping hold of that feeling of calmness within.

Other Techniques You Could Use
There are many, many alternative methods.

1. You might like to close your eyes and hold one arm out in front of you, focusing your attention on your arm and hand. Imagine that they are feeling heavier and heavier, and just allow your arm to gradually come down to your lap, without any voluntary effort on your part, as you go deeper and deeper into relaxation, so that by the time your arm reaches your lap, and its weight comes back to normal as it touches your lap, you are feeling really comfortable and relaxed and ready to go to your special place. (see page 16)

2. You could rest one hand with your fingertips just lightly touching your knee and imagine a large helium-filled balloon (what colour is it?) tied to your wrist. As you imagine that arm and hand getting lighter and lighter and the pull of the balloon getting stronger and stronger, you can begin to feel more and more relaxed. You may find your hand starting to float up off your knee as you become really focused on the pull of the balloon as it tugs at your arm... floating up and up like a feather... without your having to consciously do anything at all...

After a while you can imagine untying the balloon and watching it floating away into the distance as you become more and more relaxed... maybe carrying away something you would like to get rid of...

You can, if you like, allow your hand to float up and up, your arm bending at the elbow, until your fingers touch your face…

…and then, as your arm gradually regains its normal weight and comes back down to your lap, you can really enjoy that feeling of relaxation getting deeper and deeper until you are ready to go to your special place. (see page 16)

3. Another method is to hold your hands out in front of you, with palms facing and about nine inches apart and imagine that you have a magnet in each palm and imagine feeling the pull between the two magnets. As your hands become closer and closer together, the pull becomes stronger and stronger and you go deeper and deeper into relaxation until, as they touch, you are ready to go to your special place. (see page 16)

Then as your hands gradually come down to your lap, you can allow yourself to feel more and more comfortable and relaxed…

4. Maybe you could just take five deep breaths, counting each one in turn, allowing yourself to relax with each outgoing breath, maybe imagining breathing in a colour and imagining it spreading throughout your body as it relaxes until you are ready to go to your special place. (see page 16)

5. You could simply close your eyes and take yourself back to some place or some activity that you enjoy and relive the experience, feeling, seeing, smelling and hearing what is happening, e.g. lying in the sunshine

looking up at the clouds ...maybe imagining your favourite piece of music playing, as you feel more and more relaxed until you are ready to go to your special place. (see page 16)

6. You could actually listen to some music that you feel is appropriate, closing your eyes and enjoying the internal images and feelings that it generates within you until you feel you are ready to go to your special place. (see page 16)

Use your imagination to find the best way for you to focus internally and tie that into becoming more and more relaxed. You could use one of the methods described above or string several together to become as deeply relaxed as you are comfortable with.

Troubleshooting

The main problem people have with these kinds of techniques is that they 'try' too hard. Why not allow your conscious mind to 'wonder' what will happen and then just see what happens?

Don't worry if stray thoughts cross your mind whilst you are doing these exercises. Allow the thought to float in, and then out, but instead of following it, bring yourself back to what you were doing. Alternatively, start counting backwards from three-hundred in sevens until you feel ready to continue!

Occasionally, if you have been suppressing various sad emotions you might start to feel upset and shed a tear as you relax. This doesn't happen often, but you can tell yourself that by expressing that feeling you have dealt with whatever it was that caused it. It is a good idea then to relax again and purposefully think of a happy memory and take yourself back there, getting fully in touch with good feelings before returning to the here and now. If you feel that you have a problem that you need some help with, then please go and see a properly qualified therapist or your own doctor.

Remember that practising this skill will mean that you get better and better at it. When you are used to accessing this relaxed state you will probably find that you don't really need to go through a long routine but, with a few breaths you can slip easily and effortlessly into it.

Once having learned to access your 'right brain' or 'unconscious' mind we can now begin to show you ways you can utilise this to help yourself become an ex-smoker.

Chapter Three

Setting Your Goal

Did you know that the bumblebee cannot fly? Aerodynamically and scientifically speaking it should be impossible for the bumblebee to fly, but nobody told it so!

At one time it was thought that it was humanly impossible to run a four-minute mile. Roger Bannister proved it possible, and very shortly afterwards several others reached and surpassed the supposedly 'impossible'.

We tend to use only a small percentage of our inner resources and abilities at any one time and often we are prevented by our 'conscious' doubts from achieving all that we could possibly do. We tell ourselves, "Oh, I can't do that", and so we fail.

If we set ourselves a goal whilst in a relaxed state (in touch with our unconscious mind), we start to mobilise all the unconscious resources we need to achieve that goal and, by visualising how we want to be, we are helping our brain to write the 'programme' that will help us to achieve it.

You get what you expect to get... so decide what you want and then... go for it!

How To Set Your Goal
1.   Relax in whatever way you feel best for you and go to your 'special place'.

Make an image of yourself as an ex-smoker. Make it a 'feeling' picture and have some way of seeing the target date, e.g. a newspaper or a calendar on the wall. Maybe see yourself telling a friend that you are now an ex- smoker.

When the image is clear, go 'into' the image, make any adjustments that you feel are desirable. Notice what you smell, hear and see, and feel how good it feels to have achieved your goal of being an ex-smoker.

Gradually bring yourself back to the here and now, knowing that your unconscious mind will mobilise the resources you need to achieve your goal.

Remember that, as far as your unconscious mind is concerned, you now not only have the T-shirt, but have also worn it!

Or 2. Close your eyes and relax and imagine that you are sitting on a road in the present time with the past running off into the distance, last week, last month, last year and all the way back to your birth, in one direction, and the future, tomorrow, next month, next year running off into the distance in another.

Make an image (a feeling picture) of you as an ex-smoker. Step into the image and adjust how it looks (maybe brighten the colours, or add movement) until it feels just right. Make it as good as it can possibly be! Step out of the picture.

Take the image and float above 'now', energise the picture with four deep breaths and imagine floating up and above your road into the future and dropping the image into the appropriate place on your time road.

Float back to 'now' and come back to the here and now with the certainty that your unconscious mind will mobilise the resources you need to achieve your goal.

As you progress towards your goal you will consciously become aware of the steps that you need to take to achieve it, as your unconscious mind has now assessed the situation and knows which way you want to go.

Reinforcing Your Determination

It is useful to practise this technique each day as you approach your stopping day to reinforce your determination.

Close your eyes and relax for a few minutes.

Make an image behind you, of how you are now as a smoker, coughing and spluttering as you puff away, smelling like a stale ashtray, looking harassed, and make it a dull, unattractive picture.

Then make an image in front of you, of you as an ex-smoker, looking and feeling good, smelling fresh and breathing easily and effortlessly, feeling fitter and more confident in yourself.

Step into the image in front of you and really feel how good it feels to have become an ex-smoker, and tell yourself that inside.

Open your eyes and then close them again and repeat a few times, opening your eyes between each repetition.

As you do this the image of you as a smoker will usually become less distinct or fade away altogether. You will have that image of yourself as an ex-smoker firmly held in the front of your mind.

Chapter Four

Dealing With The Physical Addiction To Nicotine

The principle of dealing with the physical withdrawal symptoms from nicotine is to reduce the nicotine intake over a period. This period should vary according to what your level of nicotine intake is. If you are smoking twenty cigarettes a day then you should reduce your nicotine intake to virtually none over a period of fourteen days. For every extra ten cigarettes a day the period should be lengthened by seven days (so that it would be twenty-eight days for a forty-a-day smoker).

Cigar And Pipe Smokers
If you were a cigarette smoker and then you started to smoke a pipe or cigars then you should first change back to smoking cigarettes again for a few days. This will allow you to establish your baseline level of smoking before commencing the reduction process as explained above. Some do this and say that they do not like the process of smoking cigarettes. Well, isn't that a shame!? It will mean, of course, that the time when you stop completely will be such a pleasant relief, won't it?

How To Reduce Your Intake
Reduction could be achieved by gradually smoking a lesser number of cigarettes each day but this way you would be suffering psychological as well as physical withdrawal at the same time. As you got down to two or three cigarettes then they would become very precious, and you would be less and less likely to stop something which you were enjoying more and more.

The difference in our approach is that you continue to smoke the same number of cigarettes, but you smoke less and less of each one until you are just taking one puff out of each cigarette and then stubbing it out.

If you smoke more than twenty a day you may want to reduce gradually to twenty cigarettes a day or less and then reduce your intake of each cigarette, or you may wish to start reducing gradually on each cigarette anyway.

Puff By Puff

You can do this by just smoking less of each cigarette, e.g. three quarters of each one for three days, half for three days, a quarter for three days, an eighth for three days.

An even better method is to count how many puffs you use to smoke one cigarette and to reduce by one puff a day. Usually this means a reduction from around twelve to fifteen puffs to one over a couple of weeks. This also has the added advantage of making your smoking much more conscious as you have to keep a count of how many puffs you have taken.

As we explained earlier, you feel psychologically satisfied having lit and taken just one puff of a cigarette. Hence after the reduction period you have virtually stopped your nicotine intake but are still getting the same psychological support as if you were still smoking at your original level.

A Week Before 'Freedom Day'

It is then essential to continue for a full week on just one puff of each cigarette before 'Freedom Day' when you stop smoking completely. By the time you come to 'Freedom Day' you will have worked on your previous smoking behaviour in such a way as to have broken down the unconscious process, brought the process of smoking into consciousness and made smoking such an inconvenience that you are pleased to stop.

Chapter Five

The Psychological Dependency

The three most common psychological needs that smoking fulfils are relief of boredom, reduction in stress and anxiety, and lack of self-confidence.

When any of these triggers are fired your smoking goes on auto-pilot – you may even find a lighted cigarette in your hand without realising that you have lit one! We will talk about ways to interrupt this in the chapter on 'Bringing Your Habit Into Consciousness'.

Boredom

If you smoke when you feel bored then identify when this occurs and resolve to do something about it!

It is a good idea to sit down and make a list of some activities that would interest you and that maybe you always intended to get around to if you had the time. Display this list somewhere prominent so that you can go and refer to it when you are aware of wanting a smoke because you feel bored. Then go ahead and do one of them instead.

Make sure you don't just continue to sit in the same place and reach for the fags.

Stress

Stress in itself is not a bad thing – it motivates us towards activity. One man's stress is another man's challenge! The problems start when we have more stress than we can cope with at any one time. When our jug of coping capacity becomes full it only takes a few drops to make it overflow. Then we start to have anxiety, with all the physical and emotional symptoms that can be caused by it.

The adrenalin we produce whenever we encounter stress (or even when we only have a worrying thought) affects our entire body. Our heart rate goes up and we may experience palpitations, we breathe faster and more shallowly, we may sweat and feel nauseous and light-headed. These feelings are all generated by the stress hormones we produce and if we continue in this manner we feel tired all the time. Increasing stress and anxiety affect our ability to concentrate and we make more mistakes, have more accidents, and often have trouble sleeping. It has also been shown that our immune system does not function as well when we feel stressed so that we are more susceptible to colds and minor illnesses.

How To Help Ourselves Cope With Stress
Reaching for the cigarettes is not the most effective way to relieve anxiety but is unfortunately what many people do.

A better way to help ourselves reduce our levels of stress is to take regular exercise which uses up the adrenalin – like substances we produce when stressed.

Using a self-hypnotic or relaxation technique regularly not only reduces our levels of stress hormones but also allows us to give ourselves helpful suggestions to remain calm and, moreover, to increase our self-confidence.

Discarding Negative Feelings: Throw Away The Craving

By using imagery (or pictures) you can help yourself to off-load anxieties and negative feelings and get in touch with good, positive feelings to replace them. Use of imagery whilst you are in a relaxed state enables your suggestions to affect your unconscious mind and thereby to have an effect on how you feel and behave.

You could imagine walking down some steps as you become more deeply relaxed, down to a bridge over a river, and you could use this, stopping halfway over the bridge, to throw away any unwanted negative thoughts or feelings into the river and watch them being washed away... maybe throw away your craving for cigarettes as a brown leaf and, as you see the brown mess oozing out, imagine the clear water washing it away... or you could imagine using a rubbish chute, a bonfire, or tying them to a balloon and watching them drift away... allow your imagination to find the right image for you.

Giving Positive Suggestion – Verbally

You could just give yourself verbal suggestions whilst you are in your special place such as... *Each day I will become more relaxed and calm, more confident and in control. I will become so deeply interested in whatever I am doing or whoever I am with that my problems will bother me less and less. This feeling of calmness and peace, this feeling of confidence, will mean that I have more energy to do all the things that I want to do. I will see things more clearly, without distortion, more in perspective, and each day, this feeling of confidence and calmness will grow, so that as each day passes I will feel and act with more confidence... I will feel more calm and relaxed... I will feel fitter and healthier... and be able to use my inner resources to help me to do and be whatever is right for me as a whole person.*

Giving Positive Suggestion – Using Imagery

Alternatively, find some way of seeing your positive suggestions in your special place, maybe on a noticeboard, written on rocks or drawn on the ground.

You could use the imagery of a small, still pool, very peaceful and calm to represent your 'pool of internal resources'.

As you sit and gaze at the water, enjoying the sound of silence, or whatever sounds you experience, you notice that on the bottom of the pool are various stones and pebbles. These represent all the strengths and resources you already have, and you can feel pleased and encouraged as your unconscious mind identifies each resource, even though your conscious mind may not know what they are, yet. Some you may have forgotten about, and others you may not even know you have, yet, and you can begin to feel excited at all the things you can achieve with all these resources.

Around the edge of your pool are various stones that represent other positive feelings or resources that you may want even more of. Decide what you want: maybe physical relaxation, mental calmness or peace of mind, or feelings of confidence in yourself and your ability to be whatever you want to be. Pick up a stone that represents what you want (your unconscious mind will let you know which stone is the right one), study the stone carefully, noticing its shape, texture, colour and weight, and then drop it into your pool, watching it drift gently down through the clear water to settle safely and securely on the bottom.

Using these kinds of positive suggestion regularly whilst doing your self-hypnosis will gradually build up (sometimes very quickly!) your ability to remain calm and cope with increasing stress without anxiety.

Increasing Your Self-Confidence
The way you feel depends on the pictures you make in your mind's eye or the words you hear internally.

If you see yourself as worried, harassed and failing miserably to cope with your day-to-day life and keep telling yourself this inside, then this will indeed be the way you will tend to behave.

If, on the other hand, you see yourself as coping calmly and confidently and tell yourself that you are feeling like this, then this is how you will begin to behave.

You cannot hold two opposing images and feelings in your mind at one time.

Practise Daily
Practise regularly seeing yourself the way you want to be, maybe using the techniques suggested in the chapter on **Setting Your Goal**.

Just as with anything else, as you keep doing it, it will get easier and easier to get in touch with those feelings of calmness and confidence.

As well as making images of how you want to be, in trance, you can also make images of yourself in different situations, behaving and feeling the way you want to. (See **Reinforcing Your Determination**)

1. Close your eyes and relax.
2. Imagine yourself feeling calm and relaxed, e.g. whilst being at the dentist.
3. Step into the image and feel good about how you are feeling and say something appropriate to yourself in your head, e.g., "I am pleased that I feel calm and in control".
4. Open your eyes.
5. Close your eyes and repeat steps 2. to 4. several times.

Making Links

If you think of a lemon, cutting it in half and squeezing out the juice – what happens? You salivate. A visual image has caused a physical effect. This reaction is based on your previous experiences and memories of lemons. If you had no prior knowledge of a lemon you would not begin to salivate.

We all know that smells, sounds or seeing something can trigger memories. When we remember an event we also re-experience some of the feelings associated with it. Wouldn't it be good if we could instantly bring to mind a good feeling whenever we needed it? You can learn to do precisely that!

Try standing up to attention, with your shoulders back, and raise your level of sight so that you are looking up, and feel the effect of a positive link you have already built up over so many years so that it is now a part of your physiology. Try to feel harassed and anxious whilst in this position and you will find it much harder to do!

Make the muscle movements of a smile when you feel down and after a few moments notice the effect on how you feel as that feeling in your facial muscles links you back to happier feelings.

If you use a special place to go to in your mind when you relax then, after a while, just bringing this visual image to mind will get you in touch with some of those feelings of calmness that have become linked in your mind to that place.

Building A Confidence Trigger

You can build a confidence trigger for yourself by closing your eyes, relaxing, and allowing your unconscious mind to come up with the memory of a time when you felt things went just the way you wished… a time when you felt confident and in control, when you felt good inside and out.

As you re-experience that event and feel those feelings, either press a finger and thumb together, make a fist with your dominant hand, or allow a visual symbol or internal sound to come into your mind that will immediately link you to those feelings and/or that memory.

Finding A Memory

Some people have difficulty in finding a time when they felt confident, but everyone has some positive event they can go back to – maybe the first time you swam a width at the swimming baths or completed the obstacle race at school, maybe the very first time you baked a cake and it rose in the middle instead of sinking!

If you really have difficulty, maybe imagine what it might be like to climb up a very steep hill and finally reach the top, where you can see the view spread out

before you and feel the wind in your hair, or imagine what it might feel like to win a race and have everyone cheering you...

Remember that it is the feeling of being in control and of feeling confident that you want to tie into a trigger, so that anything you can do internally to increase the feelings will help. Make the colours bright, turn on the sun, make it even better than you actually remember. Use your imagination and above all, ENJOY IT!

Build It Up

Repeat this with the same or some other appropriate memory and maybe build on your trigger each time you do your self-hypnosis. Remember, just as a muscle becomes more powerful with use, your trigger needs to be used often. The more often your mind makes that link between those good feelings and your trigger, the more automatic it will become.

Doing this will mean that you have those feelings of confidence at your fingertips, to use whenever you feel you have need.

Chapter Six

Bringing Your Habit Into Consciousness

We will now describe various techniques you can use to help break your smoking habit. We would suggest you read through them and decide which ones are appropriate for you. You don't have to use them all, just the ones that would be suitable for you, but don't make it too easy for yourself!

Smoking With Your Feet
This is when the fun really begins!

First work out whether you are a left-handed or a right-handed smoker. Let us say that you are right-handed. The unconscious process of smoking is such that you fancy a cigarette, light it automatically, hold it in your right hand and then take your first puff without using your conscious mind at all. What we want you to do now is first to stop smoking with your right hand and use your left. This will feel funny and uncomfortable at first but in a few days you would adapt so that you eventually became an unconscious left-handed smoker.

So – let the games begin! You start to smoke 'back-handed', swap hands between each puff, hold your cigarette between different fingers each time and, for those who are fit enough, smoke with your feet! When you have really used your ingenuity to the full, you will be having to watch each puff to see which way to put the cigarette!

There is, however, one thing you have to be careful about, and that is 'crazy smoking' in public. You are likely to get some funny looks if people see you performing in this way. You can of course turn the situation into a challenge and ask people why they are staring at you. Then a retort such as, "But this is the best way to smoke. Why haven't you tried it?" may get interesting responses. It would probably then be better to move away quickly before someone comes to formally assess your mental state!

When And Where

You need to really bring into consciousness when you smoke and what behaviours are associated with it. Then it is quite easy to break up the pattern.

If you smoke as you drive then you could ban yourself from doing that. That sounds easy, but let's see how committed you are about the process. Would you be prepared to take out your car's cigarette lighter and give it for safekeeping to a non-smoking friend or even throw it in the dustbin? Would you be prepared to always lock your matches or lighter in the boot as you travel? If so, then you really are well on the way to becoming an ex-smoker.

You may wish to ban yourself from smoking in the lounge or even in the house.

It is also a good idea to put your cigarettes and lighter somewhere that takes a little effort to go and get them. This will mean a lot of your 'habit' smoking may cease because you can't be bothered to go and fetch your cigarettes.

You may wish to ban a cigarette within thirty minutes of a meal or drink. Please let your own imagination loose on this and let your unconscious mind throw some rocks (or even boulders!) in the path of your smoking.

It is a good idea to designate a smoking area and stick to it. You could ensure that there is no television in your smoking area so that if you want to smoke you cannot continue watching your favourite programmes.

The Smoking Diary

The next way to completely break up your unconscious pattern is to work on the start of the cycle – the fact that you initiate the process by wanting a cigarette. What we want you to do is to decide exactly when you will smoke your set number of cigarettes the next day and to stick rigidly to it.

The smoking diary should be very exact and set out to the minute. It is no good saying, for instance, "I will have a cigarette with my mid-morning drink". It should be, perhaps, "I will have one at 10.21 am".

You will see that the process really comes into your consciousness as you are watching every minute to smoke at exactly your predetermined time. Remember it is you who sets the times and so you are now not smoking because you want a cigarette but because you have told yourself you must have one at that particular time. If, for instance, you had wanted one at 10.10 am when you had your mid-morning drink on that day, you would have had to wait 11 minutes until 10.21 am.

You are now smoking not because you want one at that time but because you have told yourself you must have one exactly then.

At the end of three weeks it is quite easy to stop because you are only stopping something you have told yourself to do and don't really want to do at that exact time anyway. Your sense of mischief can really get to work on the setting out of the smoking diary.

If you like a particular television programme which runs from 7.30 pm to 8.00 pm then perhaps you should set a timed cigarette at 7.37 pm and also set it so that you could not smoke in that room. As you smoked the cigarette whilst missing your favourite programme you are giving yourself some really negative feelings about smoking as it is now starting to interfere with other pleasures. The process will then already be starting – roll on 'Freedom Day'. It will be great to stop this inconvenient habit!

Making It Inconvenient

This is the stage where we start to make it more difficult to smoke. How do you buy your cigarettes? Do you buy them in single packs or do you buy them in a week's supply as you do your shopping? We feel that when you are committed to stop smoking then it is necessary to see the buying of cigarettes in a different way. From now on we want to continue the process of making yourself consciously aware of your smoking habit.

Ten Of A Different Brand?

You should now buy your cigarettes only in single packs – ideally packs of ten. If your brand does not come in packs of ten then why not buy a different brand which

does come in packs of ten? We can hear you thinking, "I don't enjoy them as much". Guess what the answer to that one is! We need to confess now – this book is sneaky. We will use all sorts of ways to help you to achieve what you want. Sneakiness may be the additional factor to allow you to succeed where previously you have failed. How would it be if each time you bought a pack you bought a different brand? What was that you just thought? – "I really like my present brand". Wouldn't it be a shame if you didn't enjoy them as much! Remember that we are working towards 'Freedom Day' when you finally stop. Would it not be easier to stop smoking a brand you didn't like?

Walking To A Different Shop

As well as this you should make a special journey each time you wish to buy cigarettes and also, if possible, walk on that journey. Your mind may perhaps see it as an interesting challenge to try and buy from a different shop on each occasion.

The strategy of walking for your cigarettes is particularly effective in the winter when it is raining and cold, and you could go out twice a day to buy your cigarettes.

Chapter Seven

Freedom Day And Beyond

Telling The World

As soon as you start the process of becoming an ex-smoker it is a good idea to mark 'Freedom Day' on your calendar and to tell as many people as you can that you are going to be an ex-smoker from that date onwards. This of course puts the maximum amount of social pressure on you and may be a useful lever to help you to make 'Freedom Day' a successful event.

It is particularly important that you do not exchange cigarettes with others during your few weeks before 'Freedom Day'. Tell your friends that you are going to stop and also tell them on what date that will be. From that time on do not exchange cigarettes with others.

Smoking And Alcohol

Often, when drinking alcohol socially, there is pressure to buy 'rounds', and hence you tend to drink up and buy another 'round' earlier than you would otherwise, so as not to appear mean. This can also happen when smoking in company.

The reason you must no longer exchange cigarettes is that it is necessary to separate the smoking process from your social interactions.

It may seem a little strange at first when you smoke along with another smoker and do not exchange cigarettes. This is why the break needs to be made early on. It also gets the other people used to not offering you cigarettes. Thus after 'Freedom Day' they are less likely to offer you a cigarette.

When you have stopped smoking then a danger period exists when you drink alcohol in a group. The alcohol diminishes your awareness and makes it harder to resist offers of cigarettes from others. Many people who have stopped smoking start again when offered a cigarette in a pub.

Now a few words about smoking 'friends'. Most people who smoke wish to stop but are unable to do so. Hence smoking friends do not really wish you to stop and so may either consciously or unconsciously attempt to sabotage your smoking cessation. Be aware of this potential problem. Don't lose your friends but be yourself!

Mental Rehearsal

Perhaps this is a good time to get in contact with your unconscious mind again. Here we use an extension of your goal-setting procedure.

Relax and create an image of yourself in the future as an ex-smoker and just see how it looks to have finally kicked the habit. Then step into the image and see, hear, smell, taste and feel what it is like.

Whilst still in that image imagine someone offering you a cigarette and just let your unconscious mind come up with a reply to turn down the offer. It may be something like, "No thanks, I don't use them any more".

Feel how good you feel because now you really have mastered the problem.

Open your eyes and immediately close them again and experience the image whilst hearing yourself say the phrase again.

Open your eyes again and immediately close them in order to repeat the process five or six times until the phrase comes naturally and you really enjoy the feeling of being an ex-smoker.

Finally Pulling Up Anchors

Smoking is 'anchored' or linked to different times and places and these anchors in our regular behaviour serve to reinforce the habit. You may, for instance, always smoke with a cup of coffee after a meal or smoke as you drive. These anchors need pulling up whilst you are still in your smoking period or they will serve to drag you back to your smoking habit. The way to do this is to break the link in some way.

Until such time as you have established a pattern as an ex-smoker you need to break up the links with your previously automatic smoking behaviour. If you always used to have a cigarette after a meal, then from 'Freedom Day' you should do something totally different after a meal. It is no good simply completing the meal and sitting in the chair in which you would normally sit and have your cup of coffee. This would be doing everything to trigger that automatic behaviour of wanting a cigarette.

What you should do, for instance, is go for a walk around the block, wash up immediately after the meal or do anything else you wish to break that pattern.

You may have established patterns of behaviour of smoking, sitting in a certain chair in the lounge. From 'Freedom Day' move around – either move to a different chair or completely move the furniture. This is perhaps a good day to move various bits of furniture around the house so that you are in fact establishing new patterns rather than continuing old ones.

If you fancy a cigarette then you should get up, physically move yourself and do something different.

You must move from where you are when you get the feeling of needing a cigarette. Then close your eyes and see that new you, the 'ex-smoker', in that situation, go into that image and really feel how good it feels and tell yourself something positive about how you feel now that you are an ex-smoker. (See **Mental Rehearsal**)

If you go out to work or to the shops then it is a good idea on 'Freedom Day', and for a short time afterwards, to use a different form of transport or take a different route. This is because there are unconscious cues as you go to work or go about your daily business which will trigger the unconscious response of wanting a cigarette. The breaking up of those patterns means that you are not subjecting yourselves to those cues.

A Computer Analogy
(Skip this section if you don't like/use computers!)
The brain can be likened to a computer with software which runs your behaviour. You will know, if you use a computer, that if a computer expects a behaviour then it cannot be put off.

For instance, if you are closing a file, it will ask you if you wish to save that file and whatever actions you take or whatever processes you try to do with the computer it will not complete those tasks until such time as you have first answered its question, "Do you want to save this file?".

Fancying a cigarette is somewhat similar in that, if your unconscious mind wants you to have a cigarette, then if you sit there in that same position doing the same thing it will continually repeat its request for you to have a cigarette. You are, however, the programmer of your computer which allows you to break into these loops and so, by physically moving, it is as if you switch to another window of the computer and do another task.

Weight Gain

Nicotine is an appetite suppressant and so some people put on weight after stopping smoking. This problem is blown out of all proportion by many smokers who say that they had to start smoking again because of the weight gain. If one is considering health risks then smoking is an infinitely greater health risk than the additional half stone which you may put on after stopping smoking.

Your food will taste better after stopping and your appetite may be larger. If you are careful to eat the same things in the same quantity after smoking then there should not be too great a problem. Beware of satisfying your desire for sucking by consuming vast quantities of sweets. If you need something extra, then maybe you could eat fruit rather than sweets or biscuits.

Perhaps you should allow yourself an increase of, say, seven pounds for a month after cessation. You could then set your goal for maintaining a certain weight, seeing yourself on the scales using the techniques described on page 22.

As you start to get less out of breath while exercising you could perhaps increase your level of exercise to compensate for any weight gain.

All Or None

By the time you get to 'Freedom Day' your nicotine intake is virtually non-existent, in that you are probably smoking the equivalent of one whole cigarette per day and have maintained this level of smoking for some time. Hence you do not need to worry about the problems of nicotine withdrawal.

You have supported yourself through your nicotine reduction period by continuing to smoke the same number of cigarettes and hence have, as far as the emotional satisfaction is concerned, still been smoking just the same. It is important now that you simply stop smoking completely, rather than reduce the number of cigarettes. If you continue on one puff and reduce the number of cigarettes then, when you get down to a small number of cigarettes, you will find that they are very precious and you will not wish to stop completely. Hence it is important at this stage to have an all or nothing approach and say, "Today is the day on which I am free from the addiction to smoking".

The fact that you have done all the work to break the patterns of your smoking and brought it into conscious-ness makes this step much easier, because you are now stopping a conscious rather than an unconscious habit. Hopefully you have also thrown some boulders on your path to make smoking inconvenient, in that you have made yourself buy them in small quantities and smoke brands you do not particularly like!

Sponsorship

Some people find that getting sponsorship is a very good way of assisting them in achieving goals. If you decide to go along this course of action it is best to make your sponsorship 'all or nothing' rather than for a particular period. In other words you get sponsorship of a donation to charity for the fact that you have become an ex-smoker and if ever in the future you smoke again then you, yourself, have to make the same contribution to charity. If you decide that this sounds an attractive proposition to you we would commend it, as it is yet another lever to use to help you.

Freedom Day

You will have decided on your 'Freedom Day' when starting the behavioural changes with your smoking so that by the time this day comes round you will be well prepared.

You should plan that this day will be totally different and be prepared to alter your habits and behaviours on that day particularly. After a while, of course, you will develop the habit of being an ex-smoker and will develop new patterns of behaviour.

In setting the date for 'Freedom Day' bear in mind that, if there are particular life stresses at that time, then it may be better to defer the choice of day for a short period until those life stresses are out of the way. When changing a habit, if there is emotional turmoil from other causes, then it is much more difficult to be successful.

If you prepare yourself correctly you will find that in fact 'Freedom Day' is exactly what it says, a day in which you are free from the shackles of addiction to smoking rather than a day when you are deprived of your addiction. It is worth planning this day carefully and building in some pleasurable events so that if you look in the future towards this event you look forward with anticipation.

How To Stay An Ex-Smoker
Having successfully reduced your nicotine intake and then become an ex-smoker you have achieved a great deal. However, this is not the end. You still have dormant processes within your behaviour which could be triggered if you were to have more cigarettes. When people who are alcoholics cease drinking they cannot have an occasional drink because there is a great danger that this will trigger binge-drinking and allow them to revert to their previous behaviour. Hence it is extremely important that you think ahead and ensure that this does not happen to you with your smoking.

Treat Time
Why not calculate how much you used to spend each day or week on cigarettes and put away that same amount each week in a jar? Decide what treat you are going to have instead of smoking it away. Keep this jar somewhere prominent and think how good your treat will be!

The £10,000 Cigarette
If we were to offer you a cigarette and state that this cigarette costs £10,000 and ask you if you wish to buy it,

we feel that there are very few of you who would take up the offer. (If any of you would do so, then please let us know your name and address!)

However, that is precisely what you would be doing if you smoked again. Just work out what your smoking costs per week, and then per year, and then multiply that by your life expectancy (remember to deduct quite a few years if you do start to smoke again!). We have worked with many smokers who have calculated that they have in fact smoked tens of thousands of pounds worth of cigarettes. Some smokers feel quite amazed that they have let the equivalent of a £50,000 car go up in smoke!

If you do have another cigarette, then that first cigarette is likely to make it more difficult for you to remain an ex-smoker and hence you could start smoking regularly again and spend thousands of pounds. Some people have actually put a packet of cigarettes on the mantel-piece with one cigarette in it and put it under a big notice saying, "Open this pack if you want to spend £10,000". If you like this approach then perhaps you could adopt it as an additional strategy.

Anniversary Lapses

As you pass mile posts of one month, six months and one year, you will begin to feel that you have completely broken your addiction. It is certainly true that you have broken your patterns of behaviour and have done extremely well. However, remember that nicotine is a highly addictive substance and if you have another cigarette there is a danger that you will fall into your old patterns of behaviour. Many people fall foul of anniversary lapses at periods when they feel they have established their new behaviour. The work that we did to break up the pattern of smoking makes it less likely that you would immediately lapse straight back into regular smoking behaviour, but please beware of anniversaries and also Christmas, birthdays, etc. There are those who are smokers who do not understand this principle, and they may say to you, "Oh, just have a cigar, it's Christmas" or something like that. But be warned, it is definitely high risk behaviour to ever have even one more cigarette.

If, however, you were to have a cigarette at some time in the future, then all is not lost.

Take stock of the situation immediately and say, "I will not have another cigarette for the next hour" and then repeat the process as described in the next section. It is also wise to analyse why you slipped back and to use behavioural changes to ensure that you do not get back into that same situation again.

One Day At A Time
A pilgrim had made an amazing one-thousand-mile journey on foot through mountainous terrain in adverse weather conditions. He was asked at the end of his pilgrimage how he had managed to do such an amazing journey. His answer was that the journey was quite simple as he just took one step at a time. This is a marvellous philosophy on which to base one's life and the principle can be applied to very many situations. When faced with something which may sound difficult, if one breaks it down into manageable chunks then in fact it is quite easy to handle those small chunks.

This is true with smoking cessation. What you need to say is, "I will not have a cigarette for the next hour" and then at some time just short of an hour, to say, "I will not have a cigarette for the next hour". As one is successful and gains confidence, chunks can be increased to, "I will not have a cigarette today" and then at a later stage a week, etc., etc. The breaking down of the process into manageable chunks makes it much less daunting and much easier to see a possibility for success.

Chapter Eight

And In Conclusion

Having read through this book, by now you will have learned ways to motivate yourself and use your unconscious mind to help you to become an ex-smoker. We have shown you ways to reduce your physical addiction gradually, to help you break the links that anchor your smoking to different situations, and to show you ways to bring that automatic habitual smoke into consciousness. We have also taught you ways to help deal with stress and anxiety and to build up your levels of self-confidence.

By now you will realise how important imagery is to access and motivate your unconscious resources. We would like to conclude this book with two exercises which you could perhaps usefully practise.

Can you remember a time when, as a child, you played in rockpools at the seaside? Why not sit comfortably, close your eyes and imagine a rockpool, your very own rockpool. See how wonderful it is, with all sorts of little creatures swimming in and out of the beautifully coloured seaweeds and rocks. Just spend a few moments seeing the beauty of this and watching the rainbow flashes of the tiny creatures moving about freely in the water.

Then imagine dropping a cigarette into the water. At first this will sink to the bottom and the creatures will be startled by the sudden splash. However, they will soon start to swim freely around in the pool again.

Then you notice a nasty brown substance seeping and oozing from the cigarette. This is the tar and the nicotine, and very soon the tiny inhabitants of your rock pool, realising the poisonous nature of this, will flee from the poisonous cloud and hide under the rocks.

You may feel very concerned not to spoil the beautiful little world that you are observing in that rockpool, and so what you could do is to create an entrance to the sea so that, as the wavelets lap in and out of the pool, the poisonous clouds are dispersed.

It would of course be equally sensible to reach your fingers into the pool and to take out the cigarette and throw it away in a rubbish bin, vowing never to harm your world of the rockpool with such nasty poisonous chemicals again.

Once all the remains of the brown poison have been flushed away, you can marvel and enjoy the reappearance of the tiny creatures, as they swim around in their own little world which you are observing.

This imagery can be extremely useful for you to repeat, perhaps linking a phrase such as, "I don't use cigarettes any more" as you take out the source of the poison and discard it in a waste-paper basket. You may wish to think of your pool as a visual symbol of healthy life without tar and nicotine.

The Grand Finale
You may also like to do this second exercise in your head, but we find it is often more powerful to actually walk it out on the floor, so we will describe it as though this is

the way you are doing it. It is also a very useful way to help you to get out of a negative state if you feel 'stuck'.

First, stand up, this is position 1 – you, the way you are now.

Now, in front of where you are standing, imagine yourself the way you would like to be – this is position 2. Make it a really good-feeling image.

Then step to one side – position 3, where you can 'see' both images 1 and 2. From this position you are in touch with all the resources you need. You can 'go inside' and see exactly what resources you need to move from 1 to 2. Allow your unconscious mind to gather those resources and project them to you at position 1.

Then move back to position 1 and accept the resources from your 'higher self' and integrate them fully into yourself.

Then you can move triumphantly into position 2 feeling the way you want to feel, behaving the way you want to behave, and above all, feeling how good it is to be the way you want to be. Allow yourself to really experience this and then re-orientate yourself back to the here and now, bringing with you all the good feelings you have just experienced.

remember –

**You Have All The Resources
Within You To Become
The Person You Wish To Be!**

reach for the stars – not the fags!

Crown House Publishing Limited

Crown Buildings,
Bancyfelin,
Carmarthen, Wales, UK, SA33 5ND.

Telephone: +44 (0) 1267 211880
Facsimile: +44 (0) 1267 211882
e-mail: crownhouse@anglo-american.co.uk
Website: www.anglo-american.co.uk

We trust you enjoyed this title from our range of bestselling books for professional and general readership. All our authors are professionals of many years' experience, and all are highly respected in their own field. We choose our books with care for their content and character, and for the value of their contribution of both new and updated material to their particular field. Here is a list of all our other publications.

Change Management Excellence: Putting NLP To Work In The 21st Century
by Martin Roberts PhD   Hardback   £25.00

Doing It With Pete: The Lighten Up Weight Management Programme
by Pete Cohen & Judith Verity   Paperback   £9.99

Figuring Out People: Design Engineering With Meta-Programs
by Bob G. Bodenhamer & L. Michael Hall
                                     Paperback   £12.99

Gold Counselling™: A Practical Psychology With NLP
by Georges Philips & Lyn Buncher   Paperback   £14.99

Grieve No More, Beloved: The Book Of Delight
by Ormond McGill   Hardback   £9.99

Hypnotherapy Training In The UK: An Investigation Into The Development Of Clinical Hypnosis Training Post-1971
by Shaun Brookhouse   Spiralbound   £9.99

Influencing With Integrity: Management Skills For Communication & Negotiation
by Genie Z Laborde   Paperback   £12.50

A Multiple Intelligences Road To An ELT Classroom
by Michael Berman   Paperback   £19.99

Multiple Intelligences Poster Set
by Jenny Maddern   Nine posters   £19.99

The New Encyclopedia Of Stage Hypnotism
by Ormond McGill   Hardback   £29.99

Order form
*******Special offer: 4 for the price of 3!!!*******

Buy 3 books & we'll give you a 4th title – FREE!
(free title will be book of lowest value)

Qty	Title
—	Change Management Excellence
—	Doing It With Pete!
—	Figuring Out People
—	Gold Counselling™
—	Grieve No More, Beloved
—	Hypnotherapy Training In The UK
—	Influencing With Integrity
—	A Multiple Intelligences Road To An ELT Classroom
—	Multiple Intelligences Poster Set
—	New Encyclopedia Of Stage Hypnotism
—	Now It's YOUR Turn For Success!
—	Peace Of Mind Is A Piece Of Cake

Qty	Title
—	The POWER Process
—	Precision Therapy
—	Scripts & Strategies In Hypnotherapy
—	The Secrets Of Magic
—	Seeing The Unseen
—	Slimming With Pete
—	Smoke-Free And No Buts!
—	Solution States
—	Sporting Excellence
—	The Sourcebook Of Magic
—	The Spirit Of NLP
—	Time-Lining
—	Vibrations For Health And Happiness

Please send me the following catalogues:

❑ Accelerated Learning (Teaching Resources)
❑ Accelerated Learning (Personal Growth)
❑ Neuro-Linguistic Programming
❑ NLP Video Library – hire (UK only)
❑ NLP Video Library – sales
❑ Ericksonian Hypnotherapy
❑ Classical Hypnosis

❑ Gestalt Therapy
❑ Psychotherapy/Counselling
❑ Employee Development
❑ Business
❑ Freud
❑ Jung
❑ Transactional Analysis

My details:

Name: Mr/Mrs/Ms/Other   (please   specify)...

Address: ....

....

....

.Postcode: ....Daytime tel: ....

I wish to pay by:

❑ Amex   ❑ Visa   ❑ Mastercard   ❑ Switch – Issue no./Start date: ....

Card number:...Expiry date:...

Name on card:...Signature:..

❑ cheque/postal order payable to **AA Books**

Postage & packing

UK:
 £2.50 per book
 £4.50 for 2 or more books

Europe:
 £3.50 per book

Rest of the world
 £4.50 per book

Please fax/send to:
The Anglo American Book Company,
FREEPOST SS1340
Crown Buildings,
Bancyfelin,
Carmarthen,
West Wales,
United Kingdom,
SA33 4ZZ.

Tel: +44 (0) 1267 211880/211886
Fax: +44 (0) 1267 211882
or e-mail your order to:
crownhouse@anglo-american.co.uk